LITTLE ROBIN REDBREAST

AN ILLUSTRATED POEM

by

Tamara Martin

Illustrated by:
Sona & Jacob

FIRST EDITION

Little Red Acorns

Printed and bound in the USA

Layout and Cover Design: Michael Linnard, MCSD
Fonts used in this book: Times New Roman, Charlemagne Stad, Arial, Trajan Pro and Gill Sans MT.

First Edition, 2010, manufactured in USA
1 2 3 4 5 6 7 8 9 10 LSI 20 19 18 17 16 15 14

Second printing. 2014

Illustrations: Sona & Jacob

A version of the poem "Little Robin Redbreast" first appeared in Sundays in the South, 2006, *by Tamara Martin and Vernice Quebodeaux, published by Little Red Tree Publishing.*

Previous books in this collection:

Book 1: The Little Turtle

Library of Congress Cataloging-in-Publication Data

Martin, Tamara, 1956-
  Little robin redbreast : an illustrated poem / written by Tamara Martin. -- 1st ed.
     p. cm.
  ISBN 978-1-935656-07-4 (pbk. : alk. paper)
1. Children's poetry, American. I. Title.
  PS3613.A786235L59 2010
  811'.6--dc22
                          2010048838

Little Red Acorns
website: www.littleredacorns.com

An imprint of

Little Red Tree Publishing, LLC
635 Ocean Avenue, New London, CT 06320
website: www.littleredtree.com

For my husband, Michael

For my children, Aimee and Eric

For my granddaughter, Sydney Clair

Tamara

Little Robin Redbreast

Sat perched upon his nest.

He breathed a deep and

anxious sigh,

Because today was the day he'd

learn to fly.

He looked up, he looked down,

Side to side, and all around.

His heart was pounding with

so much fear

That sounds were rushing

in his ear.

He chirped for his Mother

standing near.

"It's alright my sweet.

My little one dear."

"Today will be full of wonder

and fun,

Because today you'll fly toward

the sun."

Now spread your wings.

Look straight ahead.

Once you learn to fly, you'll have

nothing to dread."

"You'll see all the wondrous

things galore.

Curiosity will make you want

to explore."

"I know you're afraid, but it's okay.

Now listen closely to what I say."

"It's important that you

learn to fly.

I won't always be here." His mother

said with a sigh.

"It's all part of nature. You must

be strong.

Life is full of lessons, both

right and wrong."

"Someday, you will be the one

To help your baby fly…

toward the sun."

LITTLE ROBIN REDBREAST

Little Robin Redbreast
Sat perched upon his nest.

He breathed a deep and anxious sigh,
Because today was the day he'd learn to fly.

He looked up, he looked down,
Side to side and all around.

His heart was pounding with so much fear
That sounds were rushing in his ear.

He chirped for his Mother standing near.
"It's alright my sweet. My little one dear."

"Today will be full of wonder and fun,
Because today you'll fly toward the sun."

"Now spread your wings. Look straight ahead.
Once you learn to fly, you'll have nothing to dread."

"You'll see all the wondrous things galore
Curiosity will make you want to explore."

"I know you're afraid, but it's okay.
Now listen closely to what I say."

"It's important that you learn to fly.
I won't always be here." His mother said with a sigh.

"It's all part of nature. You must be strong.
Life is full of lessons, both right and wrong."

"Someday, you will be the one
To help your baby fly... toward the sun."

www.ingramcontent.com/pod-product-compliance
Lightning Source LLC
Chambersburg PA
CBHW042000100426
42813CB00019B/2937